IMAGES
of America

HOWELL
AND
FARMINGDALE
A SOCIAL AND CULTURAL HISTORY

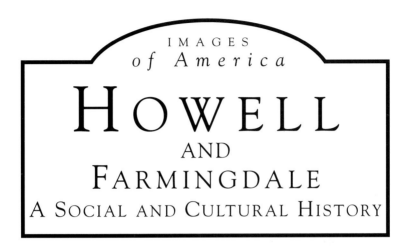

IMAGES
of America

HOWELL
AND
FARMINGDALE
A SOCIAL AND CULTURAL HISTORY

Tova Navarra

ARCADIA

First published 1996
Copyright © Tova Navarra, 1996

ISBN 0-7524-0283-8

Published by Arcadia Publishing,
an imprint of the Chalford Publishing Corporation
One Washington Center, Dover, New Hampshire 03820
Printed in Great Britain

*I lovingly dedicate this book
to my son, Johnny,
and daughter-in-law, Mitzi,
aesthetes who support my literary habits
and enrich me with their exuberant youth,
humor, and goodness.*

Contents

Acknowledgments

Very special people breathed life into this book, and to them I am extremely grateful: my dear friend *Peggy Ferrer*, who first believed I should do a book on Howell and introduced that idea and me to Arcadia; *Stephen* and *Irene Schure*, and *Lynn Dubrovsky Conley*, people with whom I attended Howell High School in 1965–66 and whose intelligence, generosity, and sweetness created a long-needed metaphysical shift in the somewhat rueful memories of my senior year; *Olia Serova*, illustrious Howell dance teacher; *Dr. Lee Ellen Griffith*, director of the Monmouth County Historical Association; *Dr. Myron A. Lipkowitz*, my good friend and modern Howell's first family physician, who provided contacts and ideas; *Dr. Phyllis Kavett*, Howell mayor of 1979 and wonderful family friend; *Beverly Lupuloff*, JCC historian; *Ruth Lane*, who sent pictures from Florida; *Eileen Wechter*, principal of the Solomon Schechter Academy; *Connie Ippolito*, of the Howell Township Engineering Department; *Bruce Fallender*, one of the greatest hearts for the arts of the Adelphia Art Center; *Gene Young*, of Young's Appliance; *Susan Wood* and *JoAnn Patton*, of Ardena School; *Jerry Carter* SH 1, USN, and *Mike Brady*, public affairs officer of Naval Weapons Station Earle; Farmingdale Councilman *Thomas J. O'Connor*; *Stephanie Kujawski* and *Patricia Irvine*, of Saint Veronica's Church; *Jo Schloeder*, director of communications, Monmouth Council of Girl Scouts; Monmouth County Library Headquarters and Howell Library and their excellent librarians, including *Judy Wolt*, *Ellen Deeble*, and *Karen Moensch*; *Anton Bremec*, of Our House Restaurant; *Rollie Feleo* and his MotoPhoto staff; *Kirsty Sutton*, senior editor of Arcadia; my daughter *Yolanda*, and my husband *John*, for their consistent care and encouragement.

Introduction

Think right, live right, do right.

—Mrs. Sarah J. Hyer

In the summer of 1965, my parents dragged me kicking and screaming to a newly built house in the Candlewood development of Howell, a 60.9-square-mile township in western Monmouth County. The population at that time was below the 20,000 mark; 5,000 more would arrive by 1980, and by 1990, Howell would have nearly 40,000 residents. The Candlewood section of Howell had no post office of its own, and we used Lakewood as our official address until well into the 1970s. Little did I know that the site of my new home had long ago been known as "Bedbug Hill," which could be seen from "Rattlesnake Crossing."

The move to Howell, one of about seventeen moves during my school years, was as close to "Bad Day at Black Rock" as I could fathom. I was doomed again to be "the new kid," a miserable adolescent who would spend her senior year of high school in unfamiliar surroundings with strangers. And in the *boondocks*, yet. After years of various residences in both urban and suburban areas of New Jersey, Howell seemed a place of exile.

Its major highway, Route 9, had only two lanes—one north and one south—before it was dualized (i.e. widened to four lanes with jug-handle turns). Locals often preferred "the back roads." To me, this "over-the-river-and-through-the-woods" route appeared to be a labyrinth. Through it, the bus took me to school, then known as Southern Freehold Regional High School. Once I was on a date with a classmate, and as we drove the back roads, he suddenly turned off the lights of the car. Very funny, of course, but there were no street lights; I noticed how pitch dark it was. I'd never been in such a rural environment as Howell in my life.

During my years as a reporter for the *Asbury Park Press*, I drove the same back roads to work. One morning, at the corner of Manassa and Old Tavern Roads, I saw an enormous pale pink pig. Grazing peacefully, it looked like a storybook pig with a sweet face. By the time I got to work, I realized I hadn't stopped smiling since I'd seen the pig. Most other times along my 11-mile commute I'd see horses, sheep, hens, deer, woodchucks, and other animals, depending on the time of day. I'd also see other drivers stop cold in the middle of the road, get out of their vehicles, and escort a stray box turtle off the asphalt and back into the brush.

I learned to love the back roads that helped one avoid traffic and similar intrusions upon nature. My favorite Howell tree, on Old Tavern Road, now part of the woods bordering the

Manasquan Reservoir, is a small but sturdy specimen with its arms up like a dancer in *attitude*. Each time I pass it, some spiritual communication tells me to let God take the reins every now and then.

Equally spiritual was a walk my friend Peggy and I took along one of the reservoir trails, when a white eagle, no longer an endangered species, landed on a low branch before us. It stayed still long enough for us to marvel. We also saw a duck sitting on her nest of eggs, a lone hummingbird, and blackbirds with brilliant red markings.

The birds and animals that frequent my front and back yards delight me, including the skunks—some of them as large as dogs. Instead of the usual white streak on black fur, some have lines of black fur on an incredibly fluffy white coat. We often joke about living in "Skunk Township." Last winter, a muskrat mom had babies in the branches of a Manhattan euonymus bush that presses against my living room window. I snapped pictures of the newborns, who couldn't see me through the windowpane. And I'll never forget the misty dawn when I was getting ready for school and heard whinnying in the backyard. A white horse that had escaped from a nearby stable was romping there!

Other aspects of life in Howell stole my heart, too. At the Universal Delicatessen, where Russian is spoken, you can find imported gourmet foods from many countries as well as Russian nesting dolls, pins, and greeting cards. The Irish shop in Farmingdale (a borough incorporated in 1903), the old Tire Farm, the oriental grocery, and the indoor Howell Flea Market add to Howell's character. I enjoyed buying gasoline at the local station run by Sikhs. A bumper sticker on a parked car there read: "Proud to be a Sikh." One can hear Spanish spoken everywhere. And I consider it a blessing to see traditional African, Asian Indian, Kalmyk, Middle Eastern, and Hasidic clothing, among that of other cultures, in public places from the shopping plazas to Allaire State Park. It is impossible to mention every ethnic group, because Howell's diversity seems infinite. Squeezing in as many aspects of the township's history as possible creates a formidable challenge in itself.

Woven into Howell's history is that of Farmingdale, once known as Marsh's Bog. Town fathers decided that the area would neither be called Marsh's Bog nor Locust Point but Farmingdale, which incorporated as a borough separate from "Howell proper" in 1903. In Farmingdale, business people made their living crafting and selling musical instruments, drum heads, bricks, and blasting powder, or by cultivating the natural bed of marl, which is decomposed marine life rich in potash and used as a fertilizer. Marl was first discovered in Howell in 1830, when a gristmill was under construction by Henry Clayton.

While marl sold for 50¢ to 75¢ a load, others relied on the cranberry bogs in Howell and Farmingdale for produce. In 1872, about 3,400 bushels of cranberries were harvested. By 1876, 166 acres of cranberries had been planted. Migrant workers, who lived in rudimentary buildings near the bogs and did their cooking over outdoor fires, picked or scooped the berries. Mrs. Addie Conrow (one of the bogs was located near Conrow's corner) had driven a horse and wagon to the bog to sell peppers to the workers. Cranberries were big business during the latter half of the nineteenth century and the first decade of the twentieth. To many, the cranberry represented one of the area's natural beauties.

I hope what remains of Howell's natural beauty and open spaces will stay as it is forever, but change is a fact of life in most American communities. The changes that have taken place and are taking place in what I now fondly call my hometown shock me at times—the dualized highway, jug handles, vanished businesses, new housing developments, disoriented deer, and strip malls. Some of the "Howell country" has been given over to convenient shopping and service providers.

Every change has some good in it, perhaps even lots of good, as I was to discover years after I'd survived high school. My husband and I bought my mother's house in Candlewood and raised our children in it. As we improved our private environment and deepened our roots, Howell itself "came of age," so to speak, as a melting pot minus the torments of a big city, and as a place with a powerfully charged history and romance all its own.

One

Howell's Namesake

GOVERNOR RICHARD HOWELL. Brigade Major Richard Howell was thirty-nine when he became New Jersey's third governor, serving from 1793 to 1801, and only forty-eight when he died. But his short life allowed him nine children, military prowess that linked him with Alexander Hamilton and President George Washington, a law degree that led to his appointment as clerk of the New Jersey Supreme Court, and political popularity as a New Jersey Federalist, with a few licks of trouble thrown in. Despite Howell's tarnished reputation as an embezzler of government funds, founding fathers in 1801 chose his name in the incorporation one of New Jersey's largest townships. Howell was born (one of twins, and they of eleven children altogether) in Newark, Delaware, on October 25, 1754, to Quaker parents. Ebenezer, a farmer, and Sarah Bond Howell emigrated from Wales to Delaware in the 1720s. Richard married Keziah Burr, daughter of Joseph Burr, a Burlington County (NJ) landowner, moved thereafter to Shiloh (Cumberland County, NJ), and participated enthusiastically in the fight against the British. His health failing, Howell's term as governor ended six months before he died.

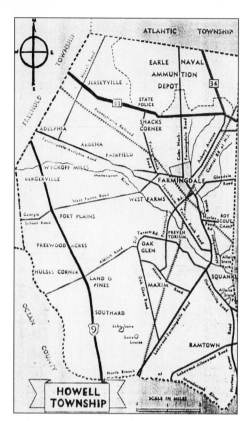

WHERE IN THE WORLD IS HOWELL? A simple map may indicate each of Howell's sections—Adelphia, Ardena, Fairfield, Maxim, Oak Glen, Squankum, Southard, Ramtown, Jerseyville, Shacks Corner, etc.—but it tells none of its stories and nothing of its engagingly diverse people. Howell Township is now 195 years old. It separated from Shrewsbury Township in 1801.

ONLY GOD CAN MAKE A TREE. My favorite tree, perhaps a scrub oak on Old Tavern Road, escaped the clearing necessitated by the creation of the Manasquan Reservoir. During the summer, the tree's neighboring foliage and its own leaves obscure its compact but exceptional majesty. Maybe a botanist can identify its "roots" for me.

Two
Diversity

THE SQUANKUM UNITED
METHODIST CHURCH. Squankum
native and teacher Sarah J. Hyer claimed
the Indians migrated annually from West
Jersey to fish and dig clams. When they
rested, they prayed for "Squan to come,"
hence, Squankum. Located on Old Tavern
and Adelphia-Farmingdale Roads, the
original Lower Squankum Free Meeting
House was built in 1834 and was converted
into a Methodist church around 1913.

THE PIERCE MEMORIAL PRESBYTERIAN CHURCH, located on Main Street in Farmingdale, celebrated its 125th anniversary in 1995. Built in 1870 in the Tudor style, both parsonage and church feature the half-timbered effect.

THE ST. CATHERINE OF SIENA CHURCH. The Roman Catholic parish of Farmingdale began in 1872. St. Catherine's was built in 1912 as a mission of St. Dennis Church in Manasquan. In 1939, the church obtained its first resident pastor, Reverend Joseph Sullivan.

ST. VERONICA'S CHURCH. Reverend Mitchell Cetkowski, the fifth pastor at St. Catherine's, found this site on Route 9 in Howell for St. Veronica's. Reverend Cetkowski became full-time pastor of St. Veronica's in 1962. (Courtesy of St. Veronica's.)

PEACE BE WITH YOU. Reverend Mitchell Cetkowski and Reverend John Reiss (now bishop) offer a blessing to parishioner Ray Barnes in 1964. (Courtesy of St. Veronica's.)

HAIL, MARY. This statue of the Blessed Virgin outside St. Veronica's rectory can be seen from Route 9. (Courtesy of St. Veronica's.)

ALTAR BOYS don their robes at St. Veronica's in 1963. (Courtesy of St. Veronica's.)

SISTERS OF THE RESURRECTION, who live and teach at St. Veronica's school, posed for this picture in about 1980. Those who were able to be identified are: (front row) Sister Margaret Mary; (middle row) Sister Mary Christopher to the far left, and Sister Cherree Power (now principal) in the center; (back row) Sister Donna Marie, second from the right. (Courtesy of St. Veronica's.)

THE FIRST COMMUNION CLASS OF ST. VERONIC'S, *c.* mid-1960s. Reverend Cetkowski is in the center. (Courtesy of St. Veronica's.)

ST. MARY OF THE ASSUMPTION. Reverend Brendan Williams is pastor of St. Mary's, which faces Route 9 in the Freewood Acres section of Howell. The mission was founded in 1950; the church was built in 1951 and reassigned as a mission to St. Veronica's in 1960. (Courtesy of St. Veronica's.)

THE SACRED HEART. A larger-than-life wood-carving of Jesus was made by Henry E. Beretta, a well-known artist/woodcarver of New York City, who created it in memory of his first wife. Beretta carved all the statuary and plaques for the church that began in the early 1900s with thirty-five mostly Italian families from New York. (Courtesy of St. Veronica's.)

THE ALTAR OF ST. MARY'S
CHURCH. A canopy of wood, painted
blue with a carved white dove
symbolizing the Holy Spirit, decorates
the altar and podium. The Alpha
(beginning) and Omega (end) flank the
Latin letters JHS on the front of the
maple altar. (Courtesy of St. Veronica's.)

ST. VERONICA'S ANNUAL PASSOVER SEDER. Reverend Brendan Williams, pastor since
1979, is shown here in 1988 wearing a yarmulke, enjoying traditional Jewish holiday food and
festivities. (Courtesy of St. Veronica's.)

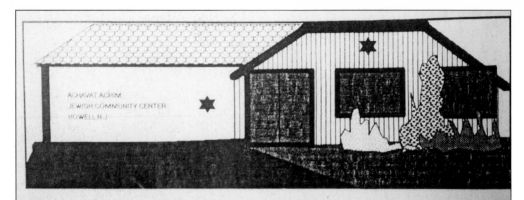

Celebrate the THIRTEENTH BIRTHDAY of your Temple on SUNDAY, JULY 31, 1988 at 5:30 P.M.

Help wish your Synagogue a "HAPPY THIRTEENTH" Birthday by listing your congratulations in the Commemorative Journal.

CONGREGATION ACHAVAT ACHIM. The first Jewish Community Center, founded in response to the social and religious needs of an increasing number of Eastern European Jewish settlers, was originally built on land donated by resident Benjamin Peskin in 1928. That building served for forty-six years until it was purchased by the state for the Manasquan Reservoir. The present building on Windeler Road was dedicated in 1975. (Courtesy of the Jewish Community Center.)

THE NEW JCC. Standing at the future site of the JCC in 1974 are, from left to right: Harvey B. Taub, Irwin Rubman (vice president), Ronald Rosenberg, Bernard Rosenberg, Carl Levy, and Gabe Sacknowitz. (Courtesy of the Jewish Community Center.)

ETHNIC DAY AT THE PREVENTORIUM. About fifteen years ago at the JCC tables are, from left to right: Carol Gottfried, Renee Rauch, Anita Albala, Iris Greene, Janet Runko, and Beverly Lupuloff. (Courtesy of the Jewish Community Center.)

GOLDEN ANNIVERSARY. The JCC celebrates its 50th year with the hora at a lively party. (Courtesy of the Jewish Community Center.)

THE RASHI LHUNPO TEMPLE. Buddhist lama Tenzing Dakpa is spiritual leader of this temple on Kalmuk Road. When encountered shoveling snow, Reverend Tenzing spoke of "opening your spiritual door." Many people, he said, keep their spiritual doors shut tight, but all the great spiritual leaders of the world spread the same word. The temple, dedicated November 19, 1955, accommodates a segment of Howell's Kalmuk community.

THE BUDDHIST TEMPLE CHOEPHEL-LING. Built in 1973 and named by the fourteenth Dalai Lama, this is the most picturesque of the three temples in Howell, which in 1979 boasted the largest Kalmuk Buddhist community in the United States. The lamas, i.e., Lamaist Buddhist monks, live in a house next door to the temple.

RASHI GEMPIL-LING, the First Kalmuk Buddhist Temple of Howell, built *c.* 1950s.

A MEETING OF THE MINDS. Buddhist monks and Kalmuks gather for refreshments and conversation. (Courtesy of Phyllis Kavett.)

SANDRA SOCHOROW, a Kalmuk woman, said in 1979: " 'Be good to your enemies' is one of Buddha's main teachings. I am a strong believer." Sochorow was one of the interviewees for an article in *Shore Affinity Magazine*—founded by Tova Navarra in 1978—which covered the Dalai Lama's visit.

MARIA BADMAEV. Maria, also interviewed in 1979, said: "Buddha was born a prince. Then he saw poverty and sought enlightenment. Part of the Buddhist faith is belief in reincarnation. If you live a good life, you come back as another person. Each life builds your character until you reach a spiritual utopia—nirvana."

THE GREAT DAY. The proclamation by Mayor Phyllis Kavett bespeaks the excitement surrounding the forthcoming visit of His Holiness the fourteenth Dalai Lama to the three Buddhist temples in Howell on October 13, 1979.

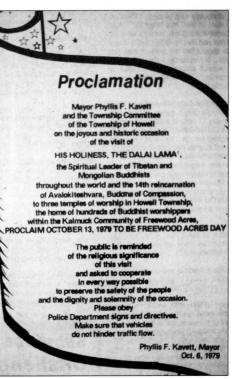

Proclamation

Mayor Phyllis F. Kavett
and the Township Committee
of the Township of Howell
on the joyous and historic occasion
of the visit of

HIS HOLINESS, THE DALAI LAMA',

the Spiritual Leader of Tibetan and
Mongolian Buddhists
throughout the world and the 14th reincarnation
of Avalokiteshvara, Buddha of Compassion,
to three temples of worship in Howell Township,
the home of hundreds of Buddhist worshippers
within the Kalmuck Community of Freewood Acres,
PROCLAIM OCTOBER 13, 1979 TO BE FREEWOOD ACRES DAY

The public is reminded
of the religious significance
of this visit
and asked to cooperate
in every way possible
to preserve the safety of the people
and the dignity and solemnity of the occasion.
Please obey
Police Department signs and directives.
Make sure that vehicles
do not hinder traffic flow.

Phyllis F. Kavett, Mayor
Oct. 6, 1979

HIS HOLINESS THE FOURTEENTH DALAI LAMA. His likeness was captured by photographer Sharon Sauer Davis on the day of his visit to Howell. The picture was first published in a cover story that ran in *Shore Affinity Magazine*, based in Howell from 1979 to 1981.

EASTERN AND WESTERN BEST. Kalmuks and other members of the Howell community of all ethnic groups, young and old, attended the festivities honoring the Dalai Lama. (Photograph by Sharon Sauer Davis; courtesy of *Shore Affinity Magazine*.)

THE DALAI LAMA, called by. American artist Peter Max "the sweetest man on earth." Here he receives the protection of a ceremonial parasol against the rain. (Photograph by Sharon Sauer Davis; courtesy of *Shore Affinity Magazine*.)

ENCHANTING SERMON. The Dalai Lama addresses his followers in one of Howell's awe-inspiring Buddhist temples. In *Shore Affinity Magazine*, writer Kathie Pitman reports: "The Dalai Lama explained that in Buddhism all things derive from compassion, and all its teachings could be summed up in two sentences: 'If you can, help others. If you cannot help, at least do not harm them.'" (Photograph by Sharon Sauer Davis; courtesy of *Shore Affinity Magazine*.)

25

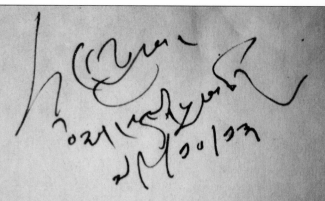

The people of Howell Township, Monmout[

are proud to welcome your Holiness to the K[

Freewood Acres. This is the largest settle[

States of persons of Tibetan and Mongolian

HIS HOLINESS' AUTOGRAPH. On the copy of Mayor Phyllis Kavett's welcome speech the day of his visit, the Dalai Lama wrote a message to her and signed his name. (Courtesy of Phyllis Kavett.)

ON THE STEPS OF RASHI GEMPIL-LING, Mayor Kavett wears the traditional prayer shawl she will present to the Dalai Lama. Beside her is the late, beloved New Jersey Congressman James J. Howard. Religious leaders of Howell also came to honor the Dalai Lama, including Reverend Brendan Williams, pastor of St. Veronica's Roman Catholic Church. (Courtesy of Phyllis Kavett.)

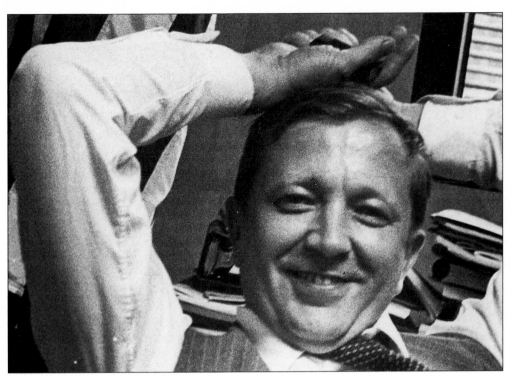

JURIS MEDNIS, a Latvian who in 1979 was president of the Howell State Bank (now First Sate Bank), said: "If our broader community cannot fully understand the significance of the Dalai Lama's visit, we can all nevertheless rejoice in the happiness and good fortune of our neighbors." (Courtesy of *Shore Affinity Magazine*.)

THE ARDENA BAPTIST CHURCH. "The first Baptist Church of Howell was organized Nov. 10, 1859, by 28 members of the Baptist Church at Freehold residing in and contiguous to the village of Fairfield (formerly called Lower Turkey). In the following September, 1860, it was duly recognized by a council of Baptist ministers and laymen from surrounding churches." (Text from the *History of Howell*, written by students of Ardena School.)

THE VAN CLEAF FAMILY MARKER, erected in 1930 in the churchyard of the Ardena Baptist Church on Adelphia-Farmingdale Road.

THE JOHN L. COTTRELL HEADSTONE. Located in the Ardena Baptist Church cemetery, this is one of the oldest stones there. Cottrell died at age twenty-eight in 1864. He was a relative of John I. Cottrell, at whose home residents of the Green Grove section of Howell met in 1854 to decide on a new name for the section. They decided on Jerseyville, the name that has since endured.

THE KETCHAM GRAVE, the Ardena Baptist Church cemetery. Ketcham graves are also in the Revolutionary War cemetery on Peskin Road and in the cemetery of Bethel United Methodist Church on Church Road. Robert Ketcham lost his life while serving in World War II.

LEFT: THE CHARLES BUTCHER GRAVE, the Ardena Baptist Church cemetery. Charles Butcher served as one of the chosen freeholders of Howell Township from 1857 to 1872. He died April 10, 1876.
RIGHT: THE DONAHAY GRAVE, the Ardena Baptist Church cemetery. Descendant Alma Donahay was a Farmingdale teacher and historian who encouraged her eighth-grade Ardena School students to write a book, *History of Howell*, which was printed and bound in the 1970s.

THE NEW ST. ALEXANDER NEVSKY RUSSIAN ORTHODOX CHURCH. Located on Alexander Road and visible from Route 9, this church provides beauty and majesty in the midst of commercial surroundings. It was built in the early 1990s for a congregation of about one thousand Russians from various parts of the former Soviet Union.

THE OLD ST. ALEXANDER NEVSKY CHURCH stood alone for many years until the new, larger church was built on a lot behind it on the opposite side of Alexander Road.

A *LANGUAGE PRESERVED* is the title of this 1979 photograph by Joseph Di Mauro of a sign
at the entrance of the old St. Alexander Nevsky Russian Orthodox Church. (Courtesy of the
Monmouth County Historical Association Library/Archives.)

FACE OF ORTHODOXY. Father Leonid
Popov was a Russian Orthodox priest of St.
George's Russian Orthodox Church in
Freewood Acres. (Photograph by Joseph Di
Mauro, 1979; courtesy of the Monmouth
County Historical Association
Library/Archives.)

A CULTURE PRESERVED captures two elders amid books and artifacts in the Russian Naval Museum in the Rodina building, located behind the old St. Alexander Nevsky Russian Orthodox Church. Much of the archival collection, unfortunately for the community of Howell, has been returned to the Museum of Armed Forces of the Russian Federation in Moscow. (Photograph by Joseph Di Mauro; courtesy of the Monmouth County Historical Association Library/Archives.)

RUSSIAN ORTHODOX PALM SUNDAY, 1978, photographed by Joseph Di Mauro. (Courtesy of the Monmouth County Historical Association Library/Archives.)

THE INTERIOR OF ST. GEORGE'S RUSSIAN ORTHODOX CHURCH, Freewood Acres, photographed by Joseph Di Mauro. (Courtesy of the Monmouth County Historical Association Library/Archives.)

THE OLDEST RESIDENT OF FREEWOOD ACRES. This portrait of a ninety-two-year-old unidentified Russian man was taken by Joseph Di Mauro in 1979. (Courtesy of the Monmouth County Historical Association Library/Archives.)

TOP LEFT: THE RODINA is the community hall of the Russian population of the St. Alexander Nevsky and St. George's Russian Orthodox churches. The Russian Naval Museum was once housed in this building, which was erected in 1954.

TOP RIGHT: *A LIFE OF HARD WORK.* remains unbetrayed by the serene expression on the face of a Russian woman, photographed by Joseph Di Mauro in 1979. (Courtesy of the Monmouth County Historical Association Library/Archives.)

LEFT: *RUSSIAN ICONS,* Howell Township, photographed by Joseph Di Mauro in 1979. (Courtesy of the Monmouth County Historical Association Library/Archives.)

RUSSIANS JUST WANNA HAVE FUN. A Rodina-sponsored New Year's Eve flyer promises a great time on December 31 and on the Russian New Year, January 13.

RODINA
234 Alexander Ave., Howell, N.J.

31ᵍᵒ ДЕКАБРЯ
ВСТРЕЧА НОВОГО ГОДА

В 9:30 ЧАСОВ ВЕЧЕРА
ИГРАЕТ ОРКЕСТР А. ОЛЬХОВСКОГО
СПРАВКИ ПО ТЕЛ. (908) 363-4062
(908) 363-9503

ВХОДНАЯ ПЛАТА
ЧЛЕНЫ 30. ГОСТИ 35.

NEW YEAR'S GALA
DECEMBER 31, 1995

Entrance: $30.00 Members $35.00 Guests
Information: 363-4062

Featuring
Orchestra A. Olkhovsky

Celebrate the Russian New Year, Saturday, January 13 - 9:00 pm

В СУББОТУ 13 ЯНВАРЯ
В 9:00 ЧАСОВ ВЕЧЕРА
ВСТРЕЧА НОВОГО ГОДА
ПО СТАРОМУ СТИЛЮ

AN OLD DRAWING OF THE CHAPEL OF ST. GEORGE, now known as the St. George Russian Orthodox Church, appeared in the *History of Howell*. According to the students' text, the walls were covered with icons familiar to Orthodox Catholics.

THE ST. GEORGE RUSSIAN ORTHODOX CHURCH, built in 1965 under the direction of Howell resident M. Lermentov, is an unexpected and glorious sight, with its Byzantine-style blue onion domes and charming entrance gate amid the unpretentious houses of Freewood Acres. The church practices a combination of the Russian-Cossack and Greek Orthodox religions.

THE FORMER ALL COSSACKS HALL still stands on the corner of Aldrich and Oak Glen Roads. Aldrich Road began near the Aldrich School as an 8-foot gravel road created by Rogers and Jack Irving in 1913. The Cossack building has been boarded up for many years now, but it provided a community gathering place for the Cossacks who arrived in the Howell area during the 1930s.

ANOTHER FORMER COSSACKS HOME USA remains in Freewood Acres, but it is used as a recreational facility by Kalmuks and other Freewood Acres residents.

THE COSSACKS MUSEUM. The entrance to the present Kuban Cossacks Corporation Library & Museum, 47–49 East Third Street in Freewood Acres, is a fanciful embellishment to an otherwise plain white stucco building. The museum, located next door to St. George Church, preserves art, books, and other Cossack treasures.

KUBAN COSSACK MEN IN RUSSIA, before the Russian Revolution. These residents of the Kuban River region are shown here in their finest clothes and regalia. Numbers of their descendants emigrated to America. Although there were once thousands of Cossacks in Howell, Jackson, and Lakewood, there are only about two hundred here today. (Courtesy of Vassily Lyashko.)

SENTIMENTAL VALUE. Vassily Lyashko proudly offered this 1913 photograph of, from left to right: his grandfather, Iley Lyashko; his grandmother's brother, Andrew Parcomenko; and his cousin, Tet Kushnar. Vassily enjoys having the photograph, which was taken in Russia, with him in America as a reminder of his homeland and family. (Courtesy of Vassily Lyashko.)

IMMIGRATION FROM RUSSIA. Vassily Lyashko (with dark hair and mustache in the top row) departs for America in 1990 from the large city of Krasnodar, capital of the Cossack region. In front of St. Catherine's Church in Russia, a Russian Orthodox priest gives a blessing as another man holds the Cossack flag. (Courtesy of Vassily Lyashko.)

KUBAN COSSACK PRESIDENT ALEXANDER PEWNEW (center), Vassily Lyashko (right), and Treasurer Nick Kartishko don their Cossack uniforms for a meeting in the museum. The Pewnews, parents of three grown children, moved to Howell in 1958. According to Alex Pewnew, the township is "the best place for outdoor recreation and to raise a family." (Courtesy of the Kuban Cossacks Corporation Library & Museum.)

COSSACK ART. A Cossack holiday gathering offers a glimpse of the paintings that line the museum walls. The same local Cossacks who created these works of art were also produce and poultry farmers, workers in the 3M Corporation (Alex Pewnew retired from 3M in 1991), and employees of the Freehold rug mill. (Courtesy of the Kuban Cossacks Corporation Library & Museum.)

ENJOYING THE SPRING DANCE at the Kuban Cossacks Library & Museum are, from left to right: Tatiana Brenjew, Olga Babeshko, and Maria Drichilo. In August 1996, Kuban Cossacks will celebrate three hundred years of the Kuban Cossack movement in Russia that began in 1696. (Courtesy of the Kuban Cossacks Corporation Library & Museum.)

DIMITRY MATVIENKO, billed as the "Hot Flaming Dagger Dancer and Flame Swallower," lived in Lakewood but performed in many venues, including the Casino Russe (Carnegie Hall Building, NY) and the Kuban Cossacks Corporation Library & Museum. Matvienko died in 1995. This Lumitone Photoprint postcard dates probably from the 1930s. (Courtesy of the Kuban Cossacks Corporation Library & Museum.)

CHIEF OF STAFF VASSILY LYASHKO and Serge Danielov stand before an Ottoman sculpture in the Cossack museum. The Cossacks fought for Czar Nicholas II in the 1917 revolution. Says Lyashko, "I'm Cossack, but I'm American and very patriotic." (Courtesy of the Kuban Cossacks Corporation Library & Museum.)

A COSSACK GATHERING. Alexander Pewnew (second from left, front row) sits next to Walter Babeshko (right), rector at the Kuban University in Krasnodar, Russia. In the top row, second from the left, is Secretary John Rimakis. Vassily Lyashko, in uniform and hat, stands next to him. (Courtesy of the Kuban Cossacks Corporation Library & Museum.)

THE ENTRANCE TO THE LATVIAN PRIEDAINE, a social club, is on Route 33. Two pillars are adorned by Latvian designs.

THE FIRST UNITED METHODIST CHURCH, on Adelphia-Farmingdale Road in the Ardena section, is accompanied by a Methodist parsonage just down the road. Other Methodist churches in Howell include the Bethesda Methodist Church, 450 feet east of Wyckoff Road, and the Jerseyville Methodist Church on Howell Road, south of State Highway 33.

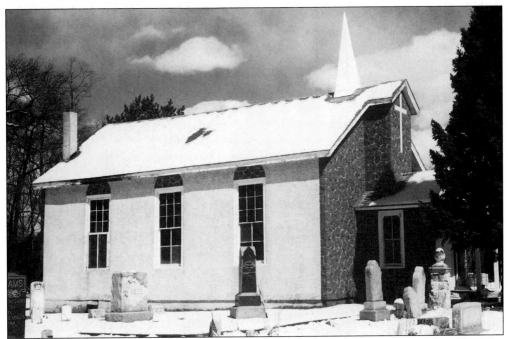

THE BETHEL UNITED METHODIST CHURCH and cemetery are on Church Road, in the Southard section of Howell.

THE SECOND GRADUATING CLASS OF 1976 of the Talmudical Academy of New Jersey Adelphia Yeshiva, on Adelphia-Farmingdale Road, founded in September 1971 by Rabbi Yeruchim Shain and graduates of Beth Medrash Govoha. Adelphia was the first residential Jewish high school and Yeshiva Gedolah in New Jersey. (Courtesy of the Talmudical Academy of Adelphia.)

GEARED UP FOR AN OUTING. Seen here are students of the Solomon Schechter Academy, Kent Road, a K-8 Conservative Jewish day school that was founded in 1969. An old chicken farm was purchased as the site for the school building originally, but the plot was ravaged by arson before classes began. The present-day building, now about twenty years old, is on 5.9 acres and accommodates 109 students. (Courtesy of the Solomon Schechter Academy.)

VISITING LECTURER. A Howell fireman speaks to a Solomon Schechter Academy class. (Courtesy of the Solomon Schechter Academy.)

ZYMRIA. In 1984, the eighth grade of Solomon Schechter Academy performed a *zymria,* or songfest, celebrating Israel's thirty-sixth birthday. From left to right are: Matthew Askin, Greg Dalia, Ezra Weisz, Leslie Parker, Cindy Mayrowetz, Erica Kuhn, Beverly Mandel, Emily Zibowsky, Gail Kadinsky, and Andrea Landwehr. (Courtesy of the Solomon Schechter Academy.)

KINDERGARTEN DAYS. Two little students have fun, c. 1988. The school's egalitarian philosophy, said Principal Eileen Wechter, includes a solid secular and Jewish academic curriculum. Ricki Budelman is vice principal of Jewish studies. (Courtesy of the Solomon Schechter Academy.)

WINNING SMILES. Students Miriam Paskind and Adam Weiss are shown here in 1988. (Courtesy of the Solomon Schechter Academy.)

Three
Education

STUDENTS AND THEIR TEACHER AT THE LOWER SQUANKUM SCHOOL, built in 1839. A new Squankum schoolhouse went up in 1879, where Mrs. Marion Stankle taught before the Howell Township schools became the Howell Township Consolidated School (now Ardena School) on January 6, 1939, with 509 pupils. A new wing was added to the Ardena building, and seven new buildings followed and are still in operation.

ARDENA SCHOOL, the consolidated school, was completed in 1938. The Lower Turkey (later called Ardena) School, originally built in 1835, measured 15-by-16 feet. Later it was used as a carriage shed at the Baptist parsonage. A new school was built in 1855. Mrs. Ruth MacDonald Smith was teaching at the Ardena building when all classes moved into the consolidated school.

AN ARDENA SCHOOL GIRLS' SOCCER TEAM. (Courtesy of Ardena School Library.)

MISS RUTH MACDONALD (top row center) sits with her third-grade students at a Howell Township school in 1939. Mrs. Ruth (Kneisser) Lane, contributor of this photograph, has identified many of the students. From left to right are: (front row) Marjorie Turgnew, Bertha Boyd, Tommy Clayton, Robert Rapp, Timmy Andrews, Patricia Gizzardi, Ruth Kniesser, Virginia Hyers, and Dorothy Anderson; (second row) unidentified, Audrey Hill, Jean Mitchell, Marion Gunther, Nellie Estelle, unidentified, Betty Burdge, unidentified, and James LeCompte; (third row) unidentified, unidentified, Siegfried Stang, unidentified, unidentified, unidentified, and Jerry Brokaw; (back row) Harry Megill, unidentified, Edith Lankstein, Catherine Dooley, Miss MacDonald, Ann Soloff, Betty Morton, unidentified, and Jack Nagle.

ARDENA PUBLIC SCHOOL NO. 2, at the corner of the Old Tavern and Preventorium Roads, was one of several one or two-room schoolhouses built in Howell in the 1800s.

STUDENTS AT A GRADUATION CEREMONY, Howell nursery school, 1954. (Courtesy of Stephen and Irene Schure.)

ARDENA SCHOOL STUDENTS ham for the camera. (Courtesy of Ardena School Library.)

ON A NATURE TRAIL, 1969–70. Ardena School students hike through a local wooded area. (Courtesy of Ardena School Library.)

SHOLEM ALEICHEM FOLKSHULE students, c. 1938, stand outside the Jewish Community Center on Peskin Road with their teacher, Dr. Boris Shegeloff (left).

THE MAIN BUILDING OF THE PREVENTORIUM, now the Howell Township Municipal Complex, opened *c.* 1910 for the prevention of tuberculosis, which had become a lethal epidemic, particularly among young adults. Governor Woodrow Wilson attended the dedication ceremony. Operated by the states of New York and New Jersey and supported by wealthy New York business people such as Arthur Brisbane and Dr. Alfred Hess, the Preventorium was affiliated with Allenwood Hospital for tuberculosis treatment.

A SIDE VIEW OF THE PREVENTORIUM reveals one of the other buildings behind it. The upstairs housekeeper, Ellen Gow, made beds, cleaned, and served meals in the 1940s. About thirty boys or girls lived in each of the four dormitories on the grounds, tended mostly by a staff of nurses and Irish immigrants from New York, Annie Layton among them. Annie met her future husband, J. Russell Layton, at the "Prevent."

ALL BUNDLED UP for classes at the Preventorium during the winter. The children, eventually numbering more than two hundred, studied, set and cleared the tables, and scraped and washed the dishes—truly communal living. This image is one of the few pictures available from the 1920s book *The Tuberculosis Preventorium for Children*, published by the State of New York.

PREVENTORIUM CHILDREN in the 1920s, from *The Tuberculosis Preventorium for Children*.

PLAY BALL! In 1988, Ellen Van Benthuysen Allaire wrote a report on the "Prevent." She worked there in various capacities until the facility closed in 1969–70. She recounted that in the late 1920s, the playground was where the Howell Library and Township Garage are today. Where the present Senior Center stands, the land was farmed, and its produce supplemented daily menus at the Preventorium.

OPEN-AIR SLEEPING PORCHES reflected the early philosophy of TB prevention before curative drugs were introduced: healthy pine air, good meals, exercise, plenty of rest, and avoidance of exposure to those already infected. The dormitory walls were not solid, but flaps rolled up and down depending upon the weather. Screens were used in the summer.

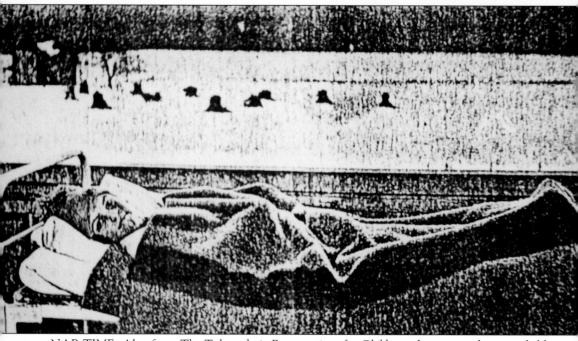

NAP TIME. Also from *The Tuberculosis Preventorium for Children*, this image shows a child content under the blankets on an open-air sleeping porch.

Four

Community Life

"THE BATTLE AX." Bernard Boyarin, one of three Boyarin boys whose family came to Howell, c. 1930s, clowns with his future wife, Minnie. (Yes, he did marry her.) (Courtesy of Lynn Dubrovsky Conley.)

BERNARD BOYARIN, *c.* 1930s, enjoys the Howell good life. (Courtesy of Lynn Dubrovsky Conley.)

THE PESKIN FAMILY on their farm, 1923, with father Benjamin, wife Rose, and daughters Sophia (left) and Mary. Benjamin Peskin donated land for the first Jewish Community Center in Howell. (Courtesy of Lynn Dubrovsky Conley.)

LOVELY LADIES. Mary Peskin (left) and Aunt Helen Friedman show off the fashions of the day in 1933. (Courtesy of Lynn Dubrovsky Conley.)

DRIVING MISS SOPHIA. Ben Peskin and family are shown here, c. 1920s, in their car. (Courtesy of Lynn Dubrovsky Conley.)

PIN-UP GIRL. Sophia Peskin in 1940 posed on her family's chicken farm for this so-called "cheesecake picture" to send to the servicemen during World War II. (Courtesy of Lynn Dubrovsky Conley.)

THE JAMES H. BUTCHER property and road in the Ardena section of Howell. This photograph was probably taken in the early 1900s, and appeared in the *History of Howell*. (Courtesy of Ardena School Library.)

THE WALTER VAN HISE HOUSE, *c.* early 1900s, on the corner of Main and Vanderveer Roads in Ardena, also appeared in the Howell history book.

ABNER THORPE'S GRAVE in Captain Matthews Cemetery (*sic*). An *Asbury Park Press* report of February 25, 1973, states that the 250-year-old Peskin Road cemetery "is part of an old 50-acre farm once owned by Abner Thorpe, a Revolutionary War figure whose body lies in the ground which was once his retirement estate." Six tombstones were stolen from the cemetery around the time of the 1976 Bicentennial celebration.

"OUR HOUSE TAVERN, 253 YEARS OLD," is pictured on an old postcard (at the time, the Farmingdale telephone number was 6-811). A famous series of murders in Howell started at the restaurant, built by Captain George Marriner in 1747 and originally named Marriner's Tavern. The tavern was the meeting place of Lewis Fenton and his sweetheart, Anita. After Anita began to show affection for another man, Fenton threatened to kill both Anita and her new beau, a man named West . . . (Courtesy of Anton Bremec.)

THE TAVERN TODAY. West and Anita could not marry until Fenton was eliminated. So, West conspired with a man who had been mugged by Fenton to kill the jealous ex-boyfriend. A member of Fenton's gang sought to avenge the killing, but was himself was killed in the process and strung up at the crossroads in front of the tavern. After that, other Pine Robbers and gang members were also murdered, which restored a modicum of peace to Howell.

JOHN MEGILL'S HOUSE AND BLACKSMITH SHOP, dating from about 1890 to 1900, was a hub of activity until horse-drawn buggies gave way to the automobile. The shop offered information on livestock and agriculture as well as wrestling mats, dumbbells, boxing gloves, and punching bags that attracted boys and young men into feats of strength. The Farmingdale building is now a hardware store. (From the *History of Howell*; courtesy of Ardena School Library.)

A wooded area near the Ardena School used to be called Horse Pound because the Indians caught the horses there which belonged to the settlers. They did this by building a brush fence in the form of a triangle in the <u>marsh</u> or <u>bog</u>. The animals were chased into this and sank in the mud where they were easily captured by the Indians.

"INVESTIGATING HOWELL." A second homemade history book was created in November 1989 by administrators, teachers, and students of Howell Township to interest third graders in the study of local history. The book, designed to be written, drawn, and colored in, was featured in the *Asbury Park Press* of June 4 that year. High school art students contributed drawings such as the one above of the infamous "Horse Pound."

DOWN ON THE FARM. Mary Peskin plays with her dogs in 1936. (Courtesy of Lynn Dubrovsky Conley.)

THE OLD JEWISH COMMUNITY CENTER, c. 1930, was popular with local families, especially that of Ben Peskin. His daughter Mary, who married a Weisgold, sits third from the left. Mary is an artist who enjoys painting scenes on saws. Sophia, who eventually married a Dubrovsky, stands at the right. She was an art major at Georgian Court College and later a music teacher in the Howell schools. (Courtesy of Lynn Dubrovsky Conley.)

THE COLONIAL-PERIOD GOODENOUGH HOUSE, at 2 Goodenough Road, was originally built on the corner of Asbury Avenue and Main Street in Farmingdale, and a Georgian addition came a short time later. Dr. Joseph B. Goodenough practiced medicine in Howell in the 1850s before he moved to Long Branch. Dr. Joseph also owned land (now Academy Street, Farmingdale) on which a $6,000 school was built in 1871. The family grave is in the Farmingdale Evergreen Cemetery.

HERE LIES SARAH GOODENOUGH. She was the second wife of David H. Conover, who kept a tavern in the Blue Bell section of Howell until 1826.

BIG SOPHIA AND LITTLE MARY PESKIN pet Lulabelle, c. 1919–20. Farmers in Howell not only raised chickens, but horses, cows, sheep, goats, and other livestock. (Courtesy of Lynn Dubrovsky Conley.)

A HOWELL NURSERY SCHOOL BIRTHDAY PARTY, *c.* early 1950s. On the right are Lynn Dubrovsky and Michael Schiff. (Courtesy of Lynn Dubrovsky Conley.)

SOPHIA, KENNETH, AND LITTLE LYNN DUBROVSKY in 1950 on Isaac Dubrovsky's farm. Isaac was a Russian immigrant to New York City and Boston and a successful grocer. The family moved to Farmingdale in the 1930s. (Courtesy of Lynn Dubrovsky Conley.)

PEARL WHITE AND CHARLIE CHAPLIN "APPEARED" HERE. The concrete remains of the Palace movie house on Academy Street in Farmingdale are shown here. W.L. Applegate Sr. owned the theater, and was assisted in its operation by his children, who served as projectionists and pianists for the silent films. The movie house opened in 1910 and was successful for a short time.

SOPHIA AND MARY PESKIN ON THE FAMILY FARM, 1936. Sophia is in the foreground. (Courtesy of Lynn Dubrovsky Conley.)

FUN AND FRIENDS. The Peskin sisters pose for a picture with their admirers. Sophia (seated on the ground) was an adventurous, athletic sort and had broken her ankle. Her crutches lean against the farm truck. (Courtesy of Lynn Dubrovsky Conley.)

THE FEDERAL-STYLE HOUSE AT 19 MAIN STREET. This 1867 home has a hipped roof, a classic doorway, and decorative brackets under the eaves. Farmingdale Councilman Thomas J. O'Connor, the present owner, heard that a young doctor once lived and practiced in the house and used cadavers for study. When the doctor sold the house to the family who occupied it before the O'Connors, the new owners were shocked to find a torso of a cadaver left behind.

ARTIST SUSAN WINTER made a painting of O'Connor's house. It hangs in the living room.

74

THE UNDERSTORY. The creation of the 1,100-acre Manasquan Reservoir in 1987 usurped land that had been well-loved family farms. Said Dr. Gertrude Dubrovsky in her 1993 documentary film, *The Land Was Theirs:* "(The land) was full of antagonism, full of love; but the community I knew is gone—it's under the water." This photograph contemplates the idea that beauty and struggle often coexist intimately, as do the tree roots and the lush moss beneath. (Photograph by Tova Navarra.)

MANASQUAN RESERVOIR &
HOWELL PARK
GOLF COURSE
Howell, NJ

THE RESERVOIR. With a 4-billion-gallon high-water capacity and a maximum depth of 40 feet, the Manasquan Reservoir can supply up to 30 million gallons of water a day. Water from the Manasquan River is pumped to the 720-acre body of water through a pipeline that is 66 inches in diameter and more than 5 miles long. This reduces the amount of water drawn from underground aquifers.

SERENITY. Fishing, ice-skating, cross-country skiing, hiking, horseback riding, bicycling, and boating activities are offered as part of the Joseph C. Irwin Recreation Area, which contains the Manasquan Reservoir.

HORSEBACK RIDERS along one of the Manasquan Reservoir trails pass through the home of upland species, birds, and waterfowl. The reservoir, wetlands, and wooded areas provide excellent opportunities to view wildlife in a natural habitat. Both endangered and protected species live here.

THE MACKENZIE HOUSE, in the heart of the Squankum section of Howell, on Adelphia-Farmingdale Road, is an old homestead that now contains the Howell Historical Society museum and library, established in 1971.

AN ALLAIRE GRAVE in the Farmingdale Evergreen Cemetery on Adelphia-Farmingdale Road reminds us of the Allaire family, for which Allaire State Park is named.

THE WAINWRIGHT GRAVE, also in the Farmingdale Evergreen Cemetery. Josiah Wainwright was a Howell Township chosen freeholder from 1841–42, and a J. Wainwright, perhaps the same man, is listed among the members of the Mingamahone Lodge (named for a local creek), formed in 1874. The Wainwright house, at 48 Main Street, was one of the first homes in Farmingdale.

ATTITUDE. Olia Serova, at about fifteen years old, danced with the Ballet Russe de Monte Carlo. A prominent dance teacher in Howell for many years, Olia Serova (Balch) was born in Istanbul to Cossack parents. She and her family moved to Paris, where she began her dance studies and career. From Paris, she went to New York. (Courtesy of Olia Serova Balch.)

EN POINTE. Olia Serova, at twelve, in a dance costume and her first toe shoes. (Courtesy of Olia Serova Balch.)

BOLERO. Olia Serova poses in a fanciful red and gold costume for one of many Radio City Music Hall performances. Here she is about fifteen or sixteen. (Courtesy of Olia Serova Balch.)

THE DUBARRY'S was the stage name of Olia Serova and her dance partner, Larry Kent. They performed in nightclubs and on television throughout the U.S. and Europe. (Courtesy of Olia Serova Balch.)

PROTÉGÉS. Long known as Miss Olia to her Howell-area students, Olia Balch instructed at least two generations of wonderful dancers. From left to right are: Melissa Elbaum, Bernadette Balnyot, Jeffrey Castro, Colleen Abate, and Sasha Tkaczevski. This performance took place in 1991. The dancers started with Miss Olia's school when they were about four years old. (Courtesy of Olia Serova Balch.)

THE BLUE BALL EMPORIUM. In November 1974, Bruce Fallender purchased the small blue building that had been a hotel in the Blue Ball section of Howell (now Adelphia). He named it the Blue Ball Emporium, and made it his home and art gallery/studio. Fallender tells of the old constable who used to sit out on the hotel steps and snag speeders and others petty offenders of the law. Young children would stick out their tongues and run before he could catch them. (Courtesy of Bruce Fallender.)

ARS GRATIA ARTIS. Inside the Blue Ball Emporium, the walls are lined with paintings and drawings. The "Fallender Fall Festival of Art" was an annual event in the community, occasionally upstaged by the neighbors' goats and pigs. Once, Fallender said, their 600-pound pig broke loose; the police, fire marshall, and humane society chased it down the street until it could be lassoed. (Courtesy of Bruce Fallender.)

THE NEW HOME SWEET HOME. After two cars on two separate occasions crashed into the Blue Ball Emporium during the night, Fallender felt "encouraged," as he put it, to move down the road in 1981 to this homestead. Also on his new property were the buildings that would become the Adelphia Art Center and the Tree Top Theatre. (Courtesy of Bruce Fallender.)

BRUCE FALLENDER stands in the Adelphia Art Center in the 1980s. (Courtesy of Bruce Fallender.)

THE FUTURE ADELPHIA ART CENTER was a small, but welcoming, structure next to Fallender's house. There he conducted art classes, art shows, and charity benefits for local artists and civic organizations. Said Fallender: "The gallery makes an effort to spotlight local artists because I've always felt that you don't have to go to the city—good art is here, too." (Courtesy of Bruce Fallender.)

AN ARTS AND CRAFTS SHOW, c. 1984. Fallender's mother, Cecilia, who died in 1985, plunked on her sun hat and enjoyed the outdoor show in the front yard of the Adelphia Art Center. Fallender's sister, Joan Riley, who died in 1995, was on hand to help and have a good time. (Courtesy of Bruce Fallender.)

A DRAMA UNFOLDS. An avid theatergoer, Fallender met a South African émigré, Andries Oosthuizen (shown here), at one of his productions at the Howell community center. Oosthuizen was looking for a place for his troupe, the Sabona Production Company, and Fallender offered him a building on his property. Oosthuizen produced *The Sign in Sidney Brustein's Window* in 1986, the first event at Fallender's Tree Top Theatre. (Courtesy Of Bruce Fallender.)

THE TREE TOP THEATRE created a funky, intimate atmosphere where Oosthuizen produced 130 plays in four years. He conducted drama workshops for playwrights, adults, and children, including children with special needs, while Fallender conducted art and music classes. Some of Oosthuizen's students have gone on to appear in Broadway productions, TV commercials, and movies. (Courtesy of Bruce Fallender.)

PLAY is the title of the Samuel Beckett work in which Margaret Rogers performed at the Tree Top Theatre in November 1986. She is in a four-foot plaster-of-paris jug made by Oosthuizen. Ms. Rogers now helps operate Oosthuizen's new theater, Amandla, on West Farms Road in Farmingdale. (Courtesy of Bruce Fallender.)

GIRL SCOUT WEEK—MARCH 9–15, 1969. The Brownies of the Monmouth Council of Girl Scouts, based in Farmingdale, smiled and giggled their way through a pilot Brownie "Heritage Hike and Trip." K.T. Kellers, a Monmouth County naturalist, conducted a tour of the Holmes Homestead and a nature walk in the Pleasant Valley area, which emphasized our dependence on the land for food, fibers, and shelter. (Courtesy of the Monmouth Council of Girl Scouts.)

THE WORLD FRIENDSHIP FLOAT. How appropriate was this theme, given Howell's diversity! On May 26, 1968, the scouts' float participated in the Memorial Day parade. The designs, one at the "nose" of the vehicle and one at the top, represent the Brownie and Girl Scout World Association pin and the Girl Scout Trefoil pin, respectively. (Courtesy of the Monmouth Council of Girl Scouts.)

THE GOLDEN CHAIN OF FRIENDSHIP, small trefoils, doves of peace, and scout flags added to the decorated float, with the girls standing on top around a large balloon painted as the globe. Four girls at the rear of the float represented four races of the world. Scouting has consistently offered educational and cultural enrichment for the children and the community for many years. (Courtesy of the Monmouth Council of Girl Scouts.)

HAO DOWN, 1966. These scouts and their leader learn to make Native American crafts and music. They wear traditional costumes as they gather outside the tepee, a conical tent made of animal skins and used especially by the Indians of the Plains. (Courtesy of the Monmouth Council of Girl Scouts.)

KARATE. In September 1982, Girl Scouts at Camp Sacajawea, in Farmingdale, practice their karate kicks. (Courtesy of the Monmouth Council of Girl Scouts.)

BLACK BELT. Master Art Beins (second from right) strikes a karate pose with his fellow staff members, instructors known as *sensei* (Japanese for "teacher") to their students. Beins founded and operates the Master Art Beins Karate Institute in Howell, acclaimed by national and international martial arts organizations as one of the top ten karate schools. (Courtesy of Art Beins.)

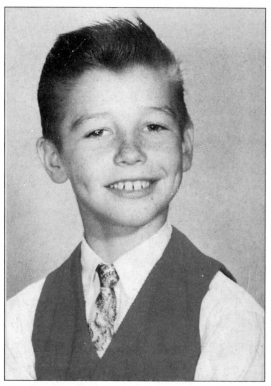

ART BEINS looks cheerful in his sixth-grade, Southard School portrait, but an *Asbury Park Press* feature story on January 16, 1995, revealed that Beins, by his own account, was once a troubled boy, headed for juvenile delinquency. Beins said the discipline of karate turned his life around. He hosts his own cable television show, and he has become a Howell luminary who has raised more than $100,000 for charity. (Courtesy of Art Beins.)

HOWELL HIGH SCHOOL GRADUATE Art Beins made a name for himself as a champion wrestler. He is pictured here (top row, third from the left) with the 1972 wrestling team, considered the best in the school's history. The school inducted Beins into its Alumni Hall of Fame. (Courtesy of Art Beins.)

A MEDICAL-MUSICAL MOMENT. Drs. Kenneth (at the piano) and Myron ("Mickey") Lipkowitz (with the clarinet) set up their practice of family and internal medicine in Howell about twenty years ago. The physicians who preceded them include Dr. Richard T. Stoutenburg, Dr. De Witt W. Barclay, Dr. Joseph B. Goodenough, and Dr. Harry Neafie, who practiced in Blue Ball before moving to Freehold.

THE TAUNTON SCHOOL BAND. Ten-year-old students of Taunton School, in Candlewood, diligently read their music during a performance for the community in 1979. From left to right are: Yolanda Navarra, Margaret Murray, Jill Zavada, and Stacey Rutter.

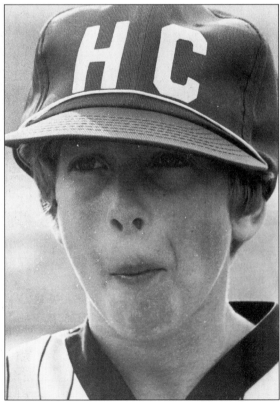

MIMICKING MAJOR LEAGUERS. Johnny Navarra, a Taunton School fifth-grader in 1981, ponders a play during a Howell Central Little League game held at the Little League field on Old Tavern Road.

THE KAVETT FAMILY on their farm on Casino Drive sit in front of draperies made by mother Phyllis out of burlap feed bags. From left to right are: (front row) the late Dr. Hyman Kavett, professor at the College of Staten Island; Diana Kavett; and Dr. Phyllis Kavett, professor of math education at Kean College and former mayor of Howell; (back row) Henry and Joshua Kavett. (Courtesy of Phyllis Kavett.)

WEDDING DAY ON THE FARM. Diana Kavett joyously tosses her bouquet after her marriage to Mark Kirsch in a lovely ceremony at her homestead. (Courtesy of Phyllis Kavett.)

TAPESTRY. One of the late Hy Kavett's intellectual and artistic pursuits was weaving beautifully colored rugs, some with Judaic themes. He is shown here seated on one of them in the living room of the Casino Drive farmhouse in the early 1980s. (Photograph by Tova Navarra.)

AN ALLAIRE FLEA MARKET. At Allaire State Park, Josh (wearing a white hat) and Hy Kavett (in his beret) set up their wares in 1977. (Courtesy of Phyllis Kavett.)

A HOWELL FLEA MARKET. A man walks his poodle through the crowds that the outdoor Howell Flea Market always drew on weekend afternoons. Many brought their pets when they shopped for bargains, "neat junk," edibles, and necessities. The large tract of land alongside the Howell State Bank that once hosted the flea market has been developed by the Union Valley Corporation.

SNOW SCULPTURE. What some might call "an attractive nuisance" because it stops traffic, others consider representative of Howell's sense of humor and fun. During the Blizzard of '96, enough snow fell on the area for the Romeos, the residents of this Fort Plains Road house, to make a monkey, er, dinosaur, of the weather forecasters.

Five
Industry, Farming, and Business

BAA, BAA, BAA. These smiling, woolly creatures on the Kavett farm in the early 1980s can't hide their fascination with the camera and the curious maneuvers of the photographer. The Kavetts bred sheep for wool and meat. (Photograph by Tova Navarra.)

THE SOUTHARD GRANGE was originally a schoolhouse built in the 1880s. Located on Route 9 in the Southard section of Howell, the grange historically served as a lodge or fraternal organization for area farmers. The word "grange" is derived from the Latin *granum*, or grain. Today, the forest-green painted grange sells produce, plants, and flowers, among its other activities.

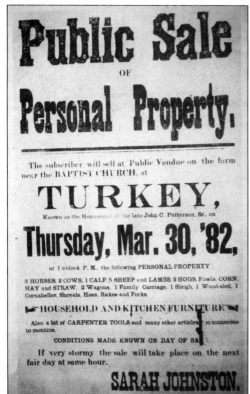

THE PROPERTY OF JOHN C. PATTERSON SR. This 1882 poster appeared in the *History of Howell*. It gives a wonderful glimpse of the items and livestock owned by Patterson, whose family was an active, prominent one. Austin Patterson served as a Howell chosen freeholder three times between 1873 and 1884, and Charles Patterson's father was a farmer who drove a horse-drawn marl wagon locally and as far away as Smithburg.

THE FARMINGDALE GRANGE. This building once served as the Red Men's Hall for the Squankum Tribe, No. 39. In the days before settlers from Middletown and northern Shrewsbury Township arrived in the Howell-Farmingdale area, Lenni-Lenape (Delaware) Indians used Main Street in Farmingdale as one of their paths from inland to the shore near the mouth of the Manasquan River.

FOLLOW THAT TRACTOR. Albert Kniesser plows his Howell farmland in 1960. (Courtesy of Ruth Lane.)

MOO-VE OVER, DARLING. Ruth Kniesser (later Mrs. Lane) enjoys her pals in 1947 on the family farm. (Courtesy of Ruth Lane.)

HE PUT THEM IN A
PUMPKIN SHELL . . .
Albert Kniesser plays with
his grandchildren, Linda and
Jeffrey Stern, in 1963.
(Courtesy of Ruth Lane.)

THE LURE OF THE BIG
WHEELS. Kniesser's
grandson, Stephen V. Lane,
wants to haul the big
pumpkins all by himself.
This photograph dates from
the late 1960s. (Courtesy of
Ruth Lane.)

THIS OLD SAW MILL near Ardena was featured in the *History of Howell*. The densely wooded areas in and around Howell made it easy to find good quality lumber. (Courtesy of Ardena School Library.)

LABOR-INTENSIVE. Early ancestors of the Schure family cut wood outside their shed, happily revealing a non-sexist attitude toward the division of labor. (Courtesy of Stephen and Irene Schure.)

A FIERCE HUG. Stephen Schure, about three years old, is shown here with his grandmother, who enjoyed the family resort on Fort Plains Road, near another camp-type resort known as Bergerville. The Schure's Acres Bungalows, once billed as a "Modern Summer Resort," still stand. (Courtesy of Stephen and Irene Schure.)

MARL'S MAIN COMPETITION. Steve DeHoff, a local minister's son, and pal Henry Kavett create a "Howell gothic" as they pose atop a pile of horse dung on Jim Roman's Casino Drive horse farm. Both boys were young teenagers at the time this photograph was taken in the 1970s. (Courtesy of Henry Kavett.)

PROUD PROPRIETOR. Stanley, the head of the Schure family, kneels beside a sign for his summer bungalows, which were rented by Russians, Italians, Poles, and other vacationers who enjoyed camping in Howell as well as activities that included parties, swimming, hiking, and riding. (Courtesy of Stephen and Irene Schure.)

AT SCHURE'S ACRES, two vacationers sit on the steps of their bungalow on a hot summer day. (Courtesy of Stephen and Irene Schure.)

FAMILY DOINGS. Children play outside at Schure's Acres while Mom does a few chores. (Courtesy of Stephen and Irene Schure.)

ALL HIS EGGS IN ONE BASKET? Not likely. Irene Weiner Schure contributed this picture of her father, Harry, who was head of the Chicken Farmers Federation during the 1940s. By the 1950s, New Jersey was known as the "egg basket" of America.

THIS POSTCARD from Schure's Acres gives the details of the resort. (Courtesy of Stephen and Irene Schure.)

SCHURE THING. The Schure home on Fort Plains Road is still a welcome respite from the outside world. (Courtesy of Stephen and Irene Schure.)

MASQUERADE. Parties at Schure's Acres brought out a creative sense of humor in vacationers. This young woman thought it great fun to dress up as a fireman, though she doesn't seem to have an ax to grind. (Courtesy of Stephen and Irene Schure.)

"I DON'T CARE—IT'S TOO DARN HOT!" Stephen Schure's mother, undoubtedly a confident woman, is caught walking around Schure's Acres in her bra. Given the big smile on her face, she must have thought the family would get a kick out of this picture for years to come. She was right. (Courtesy of Stephen and Irene Schure.)

THE FUTURE SWIMMING POOL. A worker at Schure's Acres digs the foundation of the swimming pool. According to Stephen Schure, maintenance of the resort was quite a task. At summer's end, buildings, beds, blankets, water pipes, and just about everything else had to be checked, repaired if necessary, and hauled into storage until next season. (Courtesy of Stephen and Irene Schure.)

UNIDENTIFIED CHICKEN FARMERS and their livestock. (Courtesy of Lynn Dubrovsky Conley.)

BENJAMIN PESKIN poses on his farm with women of the families that rented cottages on the property. Peskin's wife, Rose, is fourth from the left. (Courtesy of Lynn Dubrovsky Conley.)

BENJAMIN PESKIN, c. 1920s. (Courtesy of Lynn Dubrovsky Conley.)

THE PESKIN GIRLS on the farm in 1936. Ben Peskin sold eggs to Georgian Court College for Sophia's tuition. Sophia is shown here on the left. (Courtesy of Lynn Dubrovsky Conley.)

CHICKENS, HOWELL, NJ. This 1979 photograph by Rita Nannini of New York won a place in the New Jersey State Museum's show, "Stated as Fact: Photographic Documents of New Jersey," which was on display in January 1990. (Courtesy of Rita Nannini.)

CLARA ROSENBLUM seems miffed with the photographer as she gets photographed in her riding outfit, with her sister Sally and son Barry on her horse farm on Lemon Road in 1976. (Courtesy of Phyllis Kavett.)

THE ROMANO FARM, on Casino Drive, raised horses for harness-racing. (Courtesy of Phyllis Kavett.)

HOWELL STATION. Taken from the *History of Howell,* this picture dates from 1912. The original caption for the photograph reads: "Pennsylvania Railroad midway between Farmingdale and Freehold, was once one of Monmouth County's most important potato-loading centers. Old-time residents recall having seen as many as 75 teams congregated about the railroad loading platform, the activity being augmented by farmers with loads of milk. Those were the days when Monmouth was the nation's leading potato-producing county." (Courtesy of Ardena School Library.)

AN INTERESTING DIORAMA OF ALLAIRE VILLAGE, 1853. (Courtesy of the

Monmouth County Historical Association Library/Archives.)

THIS OLD HOUSE remains from what was originally of a row of eight in Allaire, NJ. It is shown here in a Johnson Brothers photograph, *c.* 1920s. (Courtesy of the Monmouth County Historical Association Library/Archives.)

AN ALLAIRE VILLAGE WAGON. About the time Howell Township separated from Shrewsbury, the Williamsburg Forge operated along the Manasquan River at the place now known as Allaire. In 1922, James P. Allaire bought Monmouth Furnace, erected in 1814, and changed its name to Howell Works. At its peak, Howell Works employed about five hundred people and had sixty to seventy buildings. (Courtesy of the Monmouth County Historical Association Library/Archives.)

THE ALLAIRE VILLAGE GENERAL STORE is framed here by the arch of the coal depot, in a photograph by the Johnson Brothers. (Courtesy of the Monmouth County Historical Association Library/Archives.)

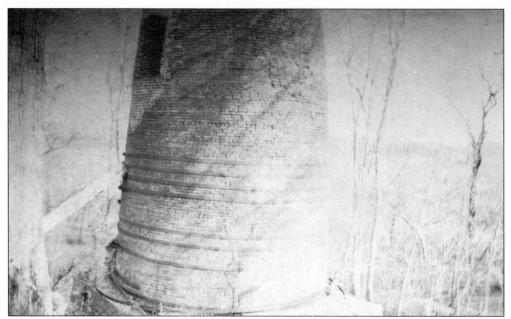

THE FURNACE STACK of Allaire Village was photographed by Dixie McKey on April 26, 1925. (Courtesy of the Monmouth County Historical Association Library/Archives.)

THE ENAMELING SHOP of Allaire Village was also photographed on April 26, 1925, by Dixie McKey. (Courtesy of the Monmouth County Historical Association Library/Archives.)

THE ALLAIRE FIRE DEPARTMENT WAGON. (Courtesy of the Monmouth County Historical Association Library/Archives.)

ALLAIRE VILLAGE, in what is now Allaire State Park. (Courtesy of the Monmouth County Historical Association Library/Archives.)

RICHMOND'S MILL IN ADELPHIA, NJ, 1923. The building is now known as Hall's Mill. (Courtesy of the Monmouth County Historical Association Library/Archives.)

CARLTON INDUSTRIES, of the Ramtown section of Howell, used to make clocks and other items. Here, Rose Giordano of Howell works on a clock face. (Courtesy of *Shore Affinity Magazine*.)

YOUNG'S APPLIANCE STORE has been in Howell since 1946 and is still operated by the Young family. (Courtesy of Gene Young.)

"B" YOUNG, c. 1960, in the store, surrounded by stoves, washing machines, and other appliances. The store's mascot is Mighty Joe Young, whose gruesome but lovable face appears on the back of their delivery truck. (Courtesy of Gene Young.)

A VIEW OF THE OPPOSITE SIDE OF ROUTE 9, seen from Young's Appliance Store, in the early 1960s. The now-dualized highway looks like a country road in this picture. (Courtesy of Gene Young.)

GENE YOUNG at eight years old stands alongside the family's truck, which reveals that their appliance business had also operated in Brick Township before moving to Howell. (Courtesy of Gene Young.)

FOREVER YOUNG. Alan, Mel, and Gene Young pose in front of the store in the 1970s. Gene remembers being taken in the 1950s and '60s to "Space City," a large amusement park with an astronaut-astronomy theme and rocket ship rides, located on Route 9 where a pool business is today. (Courtesy of Gene Young.)

ASPHALT, ANYONE? The Fred McDowell Asphalt Plant, in Howell and Wall Townships since the 1940s, combines a tremendous artistic presence with a practical purpose. The company provides paving services for businesses and homeowners. (Photograph by Tova Navarra.)

ANOTHER VIEW OF THE MCDOWELL ASPHALT COMPANY, located on Asbury-Farmingdale Road. McDowell's father originally ran a concrete business in the 1920s until he learned of the advantages of asphalt. The present company incorporated in 1960.

EARLE. In 1943, a pressing need developed for an ammunition depot in the greater New York area to support the war effort. Naval Ammunition Depot Earle, named for Rear Admiral Ralph Earle, was developed for this purpose on the border of Howell and Colts Neck. NAD Earle continued to develop after World War II, keeping pace with the changing needs of the Navy. In 1974, it was redesignated a Naval Weapons Station. (U.S. Navy Official Photograph.)

AN OLD PHOTOGRAPH OF NAD EARLE ACTIVITY. (U.S. Navy Official Photograph.)

HEADS UP, SHOULDERS STRAIGHT . . . An inspection takes place regularly at Naval Weapons Station Earle, now a compound with homes, offices, and factories, as well as a church, restaurant, community center, family service center, child development center, hobby shop, craft shop, and a laundromat. Earle is also home to rabbits, squirrels, quail, grouse, deer, and turkey vultures. (U.S. Navy Official Photograph.)

RACING WITH THE MOON. On Route 9, this sign for the infamous Moon Motel appeared in the 1985 motion picture, *The Beniker Gang*. The movie involves an orphan teen (Andrew McCarthy) who takes action when it appears his tightly knit group of friends will be split up by adoption into separate families. Who had this bit of Howell trivia at his fingertips? Dr. Isaac Siegel, DDS, whose family owns the Moon Motel and who practices dentistry across the highway.